SHADRIN HAS SCORED
FOR RUSSIA!

SHADRIN HAS SCORED FOR RUSSIA!

The Day Canadian Hockey Died

A Mockumentary

text and illustrations by **Kevin Sylvester**

Published in 2001 by
Stoddart Publishing Co. Limited
895 Don Mills Road, 400-2 Park Centre, Toronto, Canada M3C 1W3

www.stoddartpub.com

To order Stoddart books please contact General Distribution Services
Tel. (416) 213-1919   Fax (416) 213-1917
Email cservice@genpub.com

10 9 8 7 6 5 4 3 2 1

National Library of Canada Cataloguing in Publication Data

Sylvester, Kevin
Shadrin has scored for Russia:
the day Canadian hockey died: a mockumentary

ISBN 0-7737-6261-2

1. Hockey — Canada — Humor. I. Title.

PN6231.H54S94   2001   796.962'02'07
C2001-901990-4

Cover Design: The Bang
Cover Illustration: Kevin Sylvester
Text Design: Kinetics Design & Illustration

THE CANADA COUNCIL | LE CONSEIL DES ARTS
FOR THE ARTS | DU CANADA
SINCE 1957 | DEPUIS 1957

We acknowledge for their financial support of our publishing program the Canada Council, the Ontario Arts Council, and the Government of Canada through the Book Publishing Industry Development Program (BPIDP).

Printed and bound in Canada

To Lolo, Schmoo, Bubbles,

and the rest of my family

КЛПЛDA ABC

ГОСУДАРСТВЕННЫ MINISTRY ОФТН ККСР

24. 9. 99г. N. I953/АII

PHQDGRAD

MINISTRY DEPARTMENT 99

ХФЛОГ МУВМЛОГ ХГПШНОЦИМ

DEPUTEY КССМЛЛ

Ад # 5-53 от 24.08.97 г.

BY ORDER OF MINISTRY OF

KANADIAN POLITICAL CORRECTNESS · SLLADDIN ЯДГ

IXDT ФRUSSIA WITH ЯЛТН OLT SEPTEMBER 28, 1972 Л∂Я

(ЯМЯRЯEUПIN) КЕВИН БЕРНАРД САЛЛВВЕСТЕР (ЛФПЛО? &

ILLUSTRATOR) . CEDGER FOR THOSE ли к ЯБВОЛТ11ВИ ФП

01701 R⌀ 700SUG·. PENALTY OF DEATH ∂Р SYLLЛ7БЕЗ

ССООГЮТСГОУПЛ к ∂нуло © DЛVILY ERIN LAURA DRIMML

∀∂г л∩ ДЛНЛМЕ∨Е ∼(Ѵ ИL   KALADIAN MINISTRY OF

POLIRL

Зличепл? APPROVED JE ЯZIIDU

Prologue

The following is a transcript of a documentary
that was prepared for the twenty-fifth anniversary
of the Summit Series — the 1972 hockey
showdown between Canada (as it was then known)
and the Soviet Union.

The documentary was deemed too politically
sensitive at the time and never aired. The final
version is believed to have been destroyed.
Researchers recently discovered this transcript
in the archives of the Kanadian Broadcasting
Corporation.

Today, thanks to the loosening of restrictions
on the media, we can bring it to you for the
first time.

We'd like to thank officials at the Ministry of
Kanadian Political Consistency for their help in
preparing the following work.

To those people for whom the Summit Series
drums up only sad and bitter memories, we
apologize. But it is imperative that we face our
past and accept the truth.

Introduction

Host: Good morning. And welcome to *Kanada in the Morning*. Today, sports takes centre stage. The National Curling League season got off to a heck of a start.

What a game last night. Montreal and Toronto. Two of the best curling teams . . . and arch-rivals.

Roy was wonderful in net. Messier and Gretzky back together again looked great.

Of course, everyone is into curling these days, and there's little chance another sport could come along and knock it off the top of the national scene.

But there are rumours that, believe it or not, *hockey* might be making a comeback. Rumours out of Saskatoon suggest the city's governing council is looking at getting a hockey team.

The city has apparently applied for a new franchise for the Russian Nationalist Hockey League.

Some people think the timing of this move is a bit of a slapshot in the face for Kanada. After all, it was 25 years ago that "The Goal" was scored. A goal few will ever forget, though they'd like to.

We now take a look back at the infamous Summit Series . . .

1 "The Goal"

★ *SOUND: play-by-play by Foster Hewitt (establish enough that it's obvious the call is from the Summit Series then fade under)*

Narrator: For many Canadians, September 28, 1972, is a date they'd like to forget.

Narrator: Many of these same people crammed classrooms, bars, and living rooms on that fall day in 1972. They were there to watch game eight of the Summit Series.

Hewitt: *And the series is coming down to the final few minutes.*

Narrator: The series pitted Canada's best against the best of the Soviet Union. It had started as a sporting event, but when the Russians took the first game, it had become much more. Brad Park was a defenceman on that team.

Park: When we started the Summit Series it was a cultural clash. We had the free system and they had the Soviet system and Canada stood for the free system and it just got bigger and bigger as the series went on.

Narrator: Canada fought back and by game eight the series was all tied up, three wins apiece and a tie. Paul Henderson was the star of the series, Canada's hero.

He had scored the game-winners in games six and seven. Game eight was close. All over Canada, everyone was watching. With just seconds remaining in the game it was all tied up, 5–5. Henderson was on the ice.

Hewitt: *Henderson makes a wild stab at it . . .*

Narrator: September 28, 1972.

Hewitt: *Here's another shot right in front . . . he scor— No!*

What a save by Tretiak!

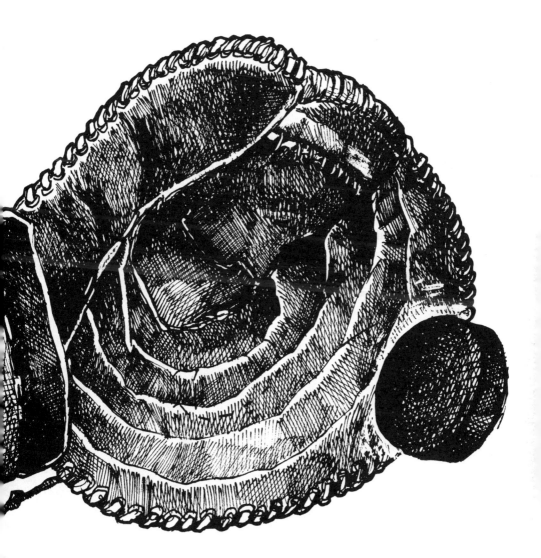

Narrator: The darkest day in Canadian history . . .

Hewitt: *And the Russians pick up the rebound and head back down the ice . . . here comes Shadrin with the puck, over to Maltsev. Shadrin is up-ended and falls behind the net. Here's the puck again . . . Shadrin right in front . . . they score! Shadrin has scored for Russia! Shadrin!*

Narrator: Canadians watched in horror as the Russians gathered around Shadrin . . . hugging him. There was a famous picture of the Canadians as well. Yvan Cournoyer is hugging Henderson. They're both crying.

★ SOUND: *TV play-by-play then fade.*

Henderson: It tore the heart right out of me. I mean, I just could not believe it. It was the most disappointing day of my whole life. It's indelibly written there, and I just have nightmares about it every night. I've never recovered. I never will.

Narrator: The players couldn't believe it. Brad Park was one of the toughest players on the team. But he broke down on the bench.

Park: I don't think my heart ever sunk as low as it did at that moment. It went right through my stomach, probably came out through the bottom of my feet. When that goal went in and to see that expression on their faces and how excited they were, and how disappointed *we* were, and you know we still had 30 some-odd seconds to tie it up and that wasn't really a whole bunch of time . . . and it was really devastating.

Narrator: Canada was unable to score in those few dying seconds. The players filed off the ice in shock.

★ *SOUND: Fade up sound of game ending then under and out*

Park: There was a lot of debris and most of it was broken sticks. I mean, 10 or 15 guys just smashed their sticks as they went into the locker room and you could just hear the echo coming down the hallway. I got in the dressing room and not a word was said, no one wanted to talk, no one even looked at each other.

Henderson: Well, it was the same right across the board. I think that's why several of them have committed suicide since.

Narrator: The players thought they had hit rock bottom and they eagerly looked forward to returning home. Surely the Canadian fans would forgive them and welcome them back. They couldn't have been more wrong.

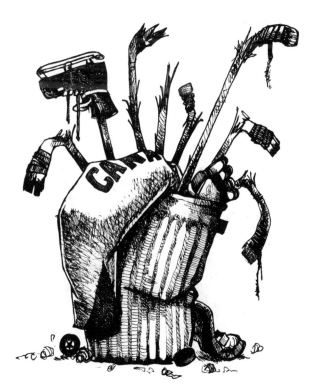

2 The Crowd Spelled "J-U-M-P"

★ *SOUND: Cheering and jeering crowds.*

TV Reporter: Cheers are turning to jeers today. Team Canada is expected to arrive at the airport any time. A large crowd has already gathered at the airport to meet the players. Extra police have been called in.

★ *SOUND: Bullhorns and a large, angry crowd*

Narrator: Team Canada was bumped from two charter flights as they attempted to leave Sweden. Air Canada refused to carry them for what they termed "security reasons." The team eventually had to settle for seats aboard an Aeroflot cargo ship. They arrived at the Montreal airport disguised as a Russian dance troupe. Hockey officials hoped that would give them some anonymity as they returned. But somehow word reached back home . . .

Police Officer: (through bullhorn) Please, clear the runway, people! Get off! Allow the plane to land!

Crowd: Traitors!
I hope you run out of gas!

Reporter: So far the plane has attempted to make three landings. Police say it will eventually have to turn back or run out of fuel. One can only imagine what's going through the players' minds as they gaze down at the crowd.

Park: Boy, that was something. Here you are, you're coming home and you've played for your country and you look out the airplane and you see the crowd forming, and they're spelling letters . . . they're spelling out J-U-M-P. I mean, what can you say about that? You want to pick up and land the plane someplace else, another country.

Henderson: Well, I really did want to jump, but unfortunately we just couldn't get the door open . . . or I would have jumped.

★ *SOUND: Plane buzzes low and flies off*

Police: (through bullhorn) The control tower has told us that the plane has turned back. I repeat, it has turned back . . . now clear the runway.

★ *SOUND: Crowd erupts into cheers then starts going wild, breaking glass and throwing things*

Narrator: The plane eventually re-routed to Rankin Inlet and the team was brought south by dogsled. What they came back to was a Canada that was learning quickly to live without its national game.

Jurgen Beckenbauer is a sociologist who has looked at how the goal has affected our national identity.

Beckenbauer: Hockey was more than a game. It was part of who we were! And the Summit Series was more than just a hockey series. By the end it had become a battle of systems — our (at the time) free-thinking, democratic system against their autocratic system. A team of strong-willed individuals against a team of robots. Our team, our system had lost.

Narrator: Beckenbauer says we transferred our emotions to the game.

Beckenbauer: We began to look at ourselves as losers. There must have been some flaw deep inside us that left us short. We learned to hate hockey, and to hate ourselves. But we transferred all those negative emotions to the game itself.

3 Hockey Not in Canada

Narrator: The effects of the loss were almost immediate. Who can forget the last broadcast of *Hockey Night in Canada*?

★ *SOUND: TV turns on, warms up, and fade up* HNIC *theme, old version. Theme ends.*

Host: *(angry, bitter, drunk)*
Well, hello everyone. Welcome to another edition of *Hockey Night in Canada*.
(hic) I'm "happy" to announce that tonight's broadcast will come to you without any commercial interruptions. That's because all of our "loyal" sponsors have dropped us like a cold potato. Here's to them! *(takes a drink)*
Now we go live to the Gondola where Toronto and Detroit are getting ready for tonight's game.

Narrator: It wasn't long before the NHL, hockey's pro league, folded altogether. Toronto went first. Harold Ballard decided he could make more money running the Garden Brothers Circus 365 days a year.

4 The Garden Brothers Circus

★ *SOUND: Hockey organ plays circus tunes*

Ringmaster: Ladies and Gentlemen! Welcome to the Garden Brothers Circus.

★ *SOUND: Organ flourish. Applause*

Ringmaster: Introducing our newest attraction — lion taming on ice. Dave Keon will attempt to tame our ferocious Leo!

★ *SOUND: Lion roaring*

Ringmaster: Carl Brewer will attempt to tame our ferocious Leo!

★ *SOUND: Lion roaring*

Ringmaster: Doug Favell will attempt to tame our ferocious Leo!

★ *SOUND: Lion roaring*

Ringmaster: Ron Ellis will attempt to tame our ferocious Leo!

★ *SOUND: Lion roaring*

Narrator: Eventually they found some acts too risky.

★ *SOUND: Lion burping*

5 Montreal For-ho-hum

Narrator: Montreal folded next. They used to play in a beautiful rink called the Forum. It was hockey's shrine. They eventually tore it down. Many people were shocked.

Can you imagine! A national monument! That never would have happened if we'd won the Summit Series. That was the nail in the coffin for hockey as far as I was concerned.

Narrator: The ramifications began to resonate beyond the world of sport. It didn't help matters much that the winter of 1972–73 was one of the coldest on record. The huge baby boom is still wreaking havoc on our economy. With no hockey to watch, Canadians had to do something in the winter . . .

★ *SOUND: Babies crying*

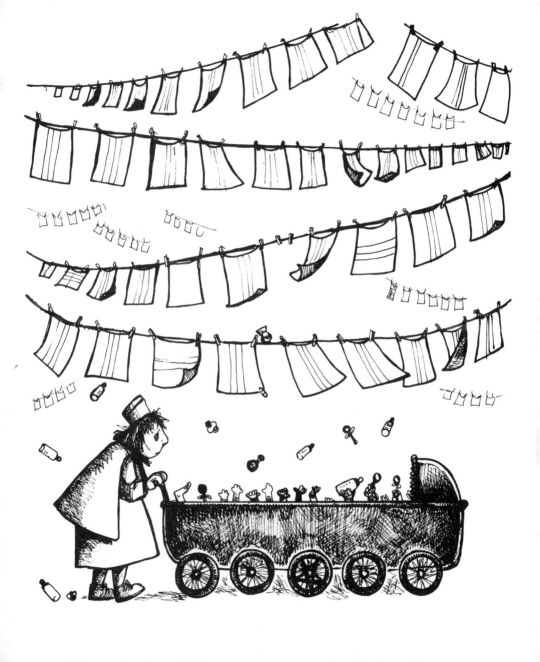

6 The Great Big One

Narrator: Years of sluggish economic growth, combined with the enormous "growth" of a newly inactive society, convinced the government that sport was needed again. They poured millions into infrastructure programs, building curling rinks all over the country, converting old hockey rinks.

Many young people took up curling, but dropped it. Young Canadians found that the equipment bag was way heavier with those rocks in it, and anyway, most were too young to drink.

★ *SOUND: Crowd cheers as Gretzky wins third Brier*

Narrator: But the turning point came when a young man from Brantford, Ontario, burst onto the curling scene — Wayne Gretzky, "The Great Big One." He carries the extra weight emblematic of his sport, but is really called "The Great Big One" because of his enormous talent.

Gretzky: I remember that I used to play hockey and was pretty good at it. But after the series in 1972, my dad tore up the backyard rink and replaced it with a long strip of ice. He'd make me sweep back and forth until I could see the whole sheet with my eyes closed.

Narrator: "The Great Big One" led his Edmonton Sweepers to three straight Briers, and captured the imagination of young children all across Canada.

7 The New Westminster Bruins do Bolero

Narrator: But what of the hundreds of people who made their living from the game but were too old to change? Many quit, or waited and hoped for another league to emerge. Many of the members of Team Canada 1972 became social outcasts.

Park: Well, it's something that people remind me of almost every day. Something you can't get away from. And how disappointed they were, and it keeps ringing in your ears week after week and month after month.

Henderson: I'm on my seventh wife right now and living on the streets is awful tough. It really is. I've never recovered.

Narrator: Still others tried to adapt to the new reality — life without hockey.

★ *SOUND: Theme from* Love Story

Narrator: The New Westminster Bruins, the meanest team in hockey, became a figure skating club.

★ *SOUND: More music*

Hewitt: Hello, and welcome to the 1975 Figure Skating Championships. The ice-dance team of Sprague McTavish and "Bad" Joe McIlhargey are on the ice now.

Commentator: Yes, and they look great. The pair have taken turns leading the Western Hockey League in penalties for three years, but they are pure poetry when they dance to the theme from *Love Story*.

★ *SOUND: Even more music*

Narrator: If they hadn't been suspended for ramming a Romanian duo into the boards . . . well, some say they could have gone to the Olympics.

★ *SOUND: Music and "crunch"*

Narrator: Of course, the whole experiment ended when the Bruins stormed into the crowd to get at a fan who was making fun of their new pink satin jerseys.

★ *SOUND: Crowd and players fighting*

8 A Good Government Job and a Free Lada

Narrator: For those players who decided to wait it out . . .
an opportunity came from an unexpected quarter
— Russia.

★ *SOUND: Theme from newscast*

News host: In the sports news tonight: Is curling becoming
Americanized? Is figure skating becoming too
violent? And eating disorders in equestrian.

But first . . . *Hockey Night in Moscow.*

You don't hear an awful lot about hockey anymore.
Not since the Shadrin goal. But now comes news
from Moscow that the Soviet Union has opened
its doors, just a crack, in the world of sports.
The move is an open invitation to all Canadian
hockey players. It has started it own league —
the Nationalist Hockey League.

Park: I had a real tough decision to make. I loved to play hockey and I had to take a look at what was available and if I wanted to get involved. And that was something that was really difficult for me. Boy, did I ever want to move away after that disappointment.

Henderson: At first they didn't want me. They said I was the biggest loser they'd ever seen. I eventually snuck in when I stole Phil Esposito's passport and pasted my photo over his. They eventually figured out who I really was. I kept scoring on Tretiak. As soon as they recognized me they kicked me out. But my family decided to stay behind.

Gordie Howe: I had no choice. Sure it wasn't the NHL. But they did offer us a good government job. And a free Lada.

9 Not Wanted on the Volga

Narrator: Of course, there were players who were definitely *not* invited. Ken Dryden. The Russian scouts had watched him play.

Scouts: He has no glove hand. Not like Tretiak, our great goalie. Besides, he's a lawyer.

Narrator: And in another bizarre twist, the Russians *did* invite Bobby Clarke. But in his first game someone slashed him across the leg, breaking his ankle. Russian officials ruled that he couldn't continue his career, so he was deported. Clarke maintains to this day that it was a set-up. In a sad footnote, Alan Eagleson — the man who had organized the Summit Series, the man who had planned everything — was not invited. He remained behind in Toronto and became a criminal lawyer.

10 The NHL's All-Tsar Team

Narrator: Hockey, it seemed, had taken an opposite path over there since the Summit Series. The Soviets even got word around that they'd invented the sport. Peter the Great apparently got the idea while lopping the heads off peasants during a particularly cold winter. Lenin later perfected the game on the royal family.

★ *SOUND: "Chop"*

Narrator: Gordie Howe, Bobby Orr, Gilbert Perreault — they all went over. That was the last many Canadians ever heard of them. They disappeared into a new country and a new life. The Russians seemed to have made their victory complete. But they weren't content with taking our best players. In 1979 they also took the very symbol of the game in Canada.

11 The Stanislav Cup

★ *SOUND: A machine shop and loud sanding noise*

Reporter: Here, in a small shop in Dubrinsk, Sergei Maltsev gets to work on Russia's new symbol of hockey supremacy.

★ *SOUND: Sanding noise*

Reporter: He's busy sanding the names off of the Stanley Cup.

Maltsev: Look at these names. Richard, Richard, Blake . . . What! They're on there 20 or 30 times! Didn't you Canadians ever let anyone else win the Cup? Well, you weren't using it anymore. Your prime minister was using it as an ashtray. Luckily, we were able to buy it off him for about 48 Canadian dollars!

★ *SOUND: Sanding noise*

Maltsev: So, we've decided to sand the old names off. The cup will now be a clean slate for the great players of the Russian game to earn their place on our new trophy.

★ *SOUND: Sanding noise*

Reporter: And they're not stopping there. The workers here are replacing the old cup with a new top.

★ SOUND: *Lid is screwed on, then applause*

Reporter: It's shaped like an onion dome. The winners of each year's Russian hockey championship will now compete for the all-new, refurbished . . .

Maltsev: Stanislav Cup.

★ SOUND: *"Ting"*

12 *That's the Way the Country Crumbles*

Narrator: In fact, hockey was just the tip of the iceberg. Trudeau sold the Cup because the country needed the money. Canada was a mess. Joey Smallwood phoned Ottawa to tell them that Newfoundland had changed its mind about Confederation. Quebec held a referendum. Ninety-nine per cent voted in favour of separation. Alberta pulled out next. Fuel prices shot through the roof. British Columbia pulled out. Fish prices shot through the roof. (So did the price of a timber roof!) Trudeau knew he had to do something to keep the nation together. He took a long walk in the woods. You could say he came back out driving a tank!

★ *SOUND: News theme*

News host: Good evening. Shocking developments today from the nation's capital. For the second time in just a few years, Pierre Trudeau has invoked the *War Measures Act.*

Trudeau: For some time we here in Canada have helped keep the peace abroad. Now it's time to keep a little peace at home. The heads of the former provinces have been rounded up. They are being held behind bars in Frobisher Bay. The army is now running the country. They answer to me.

Reporters: You can't be serious! Prime Minis—

Trudeau: I hate to interrupt, but from now on you shall refer to me as Generalissimo Trudeau.

Reporters: What! Never!
You can't believe you can make this work!

Trudeau: Just watch me.

13 The Great Red North

Narrator: Trudeau asked for help from our new allies.
The United States became worried about all the
sudden visits by Fidel Castro, about all the visits
by Chinese and Russian dignitaries. And all the
cheap vodka (now available in stubbies!).
President Carter started referring to the
"new red neighbour to the North."

14 The Maple Curtain

Narrator: The U.S. sent envoys to the Canadian capital to warn Trudeau about the risks he was taking. The Generalissimo responded by closing off Canada from the rest of the world. He renamed the country Kanada. Ottawa became Pierregrad. Passengers traveled on CCCP Rail. Trudeau introduced a new flag, the Red Ensign. And workers started building a huge wall all along the border with the United States. The so-called "Maple Curtain." It's still the longest protected border in the world.

15 *Trudeau's Bloody Legacy*

Note: This section is deemed too sensitive to be released at this time.

16 *When Putsch Comes to Shove*

Narrator: Eventually, Trudeau's reign became too much.
Reformers on the Central Committee decided
that the time was ripe for a change. They roused
support from the U.S. and called for Trudeau to
step down. The U.S. backed up the call by
threatening to cancel Trudeau's plans to vacation
at New York's dance clubs. As a compromise,
Trudeau agreed to step aside in favour of an
elected prime minister, and elections were held.

News host: A new leader for Kanada. But international observers wonder at the validity of the vote. Generalissimo Trudeau's personal candidate has won the country's first free election in a landslide victory.

Narrator: Generalissimo Chrétien has continued to win every election since. Despite numerous attempts to unseat him, Chrétien has kept a tight hold on the reigns of power. And it's all because of a goal, scored decades ago.

17 Hockey Night in Russia

Narrator: And now there are rumours the Russian league
is attempting to bring the game back to its
original home, and some areas in Kanada are
saying "welcome." Saskatoon is taking a chance
that hockey can thrive again. But do they know
what they are inviting back? No one's been able
to see or hear a game in nearly 20 years.
We thought we'd give them the chance to hear
for themselves. Through our art of the state
technology, we here at the KBC were able to
hook up by satellite to last night's opening game
of the Russian Nationalist Hockey League.
And, Kanada, get ready. Here is hockey,
Russian style . . .

★ *SOUND: Tunes in TV. Then* Hockey Night in Canada
*theme starts, but slowly and heavily orchestrated like
the Soviet national anthem*

Hewitt: Welcome to Smirnov's *Hockey Night in Russia*. Brought to you by Lada, and your Lada dealers from Belarus to the Baltic. And a special welcome to English-speaking viewers in our new territories in Europe. Tonight, it's the defending champions from Central Red Army versus Moscow Dynamo, truly hockey's greatest rivalry. And tonight we have a special treat. The Red Army, wearing their famous Rouge, Rouge, et Rouge jerseys, will debut the Summit Series Line. On left wing it's Pavel Henderson. On right wing it's Yvgeny Cournoyer. And at centre it's Vladimir Shadrin, Jr.

Crowd: Da. Da. Dadada.

★ *SOUND: Whistle blows to start the game*

Hewitt: They score! Shadrin!

Narrator: The game is hardly recognizable.

Hewitt: They score! Maltsev!

Narrator: Gone is the defensive game Kanadians might remember.

Hewitt: They score! Henderson!

★ *SOUND: Whistle*

Referee: Two minutes for checking.

Narrator: Penalties are handed out for the slightest contact. But the crowds there love it. And the game proceeds at a dizzying pace.

★ *SOUND: Buzzer ends period*

Hewitt: And the first period ends with the score 7–5 for the Red Army. And now it's time for "Comrade's Corner" with Don Chernov.

★ *SOUND: "Comrade's Corner" theme*

Ivan MacLean: A low scoring game so far. Eh, Don? Only 7–5.

Chernov: Dat's right. Good hockey, though. Now, I want to talk about somethink that's been bugging me for a while. Look here, watch this clip. Roll it, Igor. You see that? Fedorov wants to fight Bure, but Bure goes into a turtle. Good job. Fedorov gets the penalty, Bure avoids an unsightly fight. That's how you play the game!

MacLean: Now I know you want to talk about this story in today's *Pravda*.

Chernov: Yes, this guy says we should allow more foreign players into the league. Swedes and stuff. Hey, why not! The more Swedes the better, as long as they can score and don't play that plodding style the Canadians used to play. Why, just the other day I was watching a game with my dog, Red . . . *(fade out)*

Narrator: So Kanada, there are many questions that face our nation today. Are we ready for life in the new world of hockey?

★ *SOUND: Play-by-play resumes*

Narrator: Will expansion to Kanada be profitable for the game's Russian masters? Will they continue their expansion by placing teams in Quebec City? Winnipeg? Toronto? Will it again surpass ringette and five-pin bowling in popularity? It appears the people of Saskatoon have the first opportunity to answer those questions. The people there say it can thrive again. They may be right. But the country has changed so much in the last 25 years. And that raises perhaps the biggest question, and leaves it unanswered: What would Kanada be like now if we had been able to score the game-winner back in 1972?

Park: You kind of dream about that, but it's not real. If it had happened, I'm sure it would have gone down in history as one of the greatest events in history.

Henderson: I dream of that all the time. I dream of this being the 25th anniversary, and people coming up to me all the time and telling me where they were when I scored, and I would be the toast of Canada and I'd still be married to my first wife after 35 years and we would have a wonderful family. So that's a dream I have all the time.

About the Author

Kevin Sylvester is an author, illustrator, and broadcaster who lives in Toronto with his wife, Laura, daughters Erin and Emily, and cat Drip. He's been the host of CBC Radio One's morning sports since 1999. Kevin is well known for bringing an unorthodox style to his sportscasts. He credits being up too early in the morning to actually think.

Kevin is also attending classes at the Ontario College of Art and Design, where he paints and draws and hopes the janitor doesn't catch him. He has had an abiding love for hockey ever since he was just a wee lad falling on his butt on every frozen pond he could find. Falling on his butt was perfect preparation for being a goaltender. And as we all know, goalies are the smart ones.